# Hurricanes

## Catherine Chambers

Heinemann

www.heinemann.co.uk
Visit our website to find out more information about Heinemann Library books.

To order:
☎ Phone 44 (0) 1865 888066
▤ Send a fax to 44 (0) 1865 314091
▢ Visit the Heinemann Bookshop at www.heinemann.co.uk to browse our catalogue and order online.

First published in Great Britain by Heinemann Library, Halley Court, Jordan Hill, Oxford OX2 8EJ
a division of Reed Educational and Professional Publishing Ltd. Heinemann is a registered trademark of Reed Educational & Professional Publishing Ltd.

OXFORD MELBOURNE AUCKLAND JOHANNESBURG BLANTYRE
GABORONE IBADAN PORTSMOUTH (NH) USA CHICAGO

© Reed Educational and Professional Publishing Ltd 2000
The moral right of the proprietor has been asserted.

Designed by Celia Floyd
Originated by Dot Gradations
Printed by Wing King Tong, in Hong Kong

ISBN 0 431 09600 7 (hardback)
03 02 01 00
10 9 8 7 6 5 4 3 2 1

ISBN 0 431 09607 4 (paperback)
04 03 02 01
10 9 8 7 6 5 4 3 2 1

**British Library Cataloguing in Publication Data**

Chambers, Catherine
Hurricane. – (Disasters in Nature)
1. Hurricanes – Juvenile literature
I. Title
551.5'52

**Acknowledgements**

The Publishers would like to thank the following for permission to reproduce photographs:

*Ardea*: Richard Vaughan pg.45; *BBC Natural History Unit*: Michael & Patricia Fogden pg.42, M W Richards pg.21, Mike Wilkes pg.15; *Colorific*: Cindy Karp pg.11, Lori Grinker/Contact pg.33; *Corbis*: pg.38; *FLPA*: D Hoadley pg.8, Jurgen & Christine Sohns pg.43, M Nimmo pg.25, Robert Steinau pg.27, Roger Wilmshurst pg.12; *Hulton Getty*: pg.13; *Katz Pictures*: p.36; *NHPA*: A.N.T. pg.34, Alan Williams pg.25, Kevin Schafer pg.40; *Panos*: Neil Cooper pg.35, Pedro Guzman pg.9; *Photri*: pg.23, pg.31; *Pictor*: pg.10, pg.37; *Planet Earth Pictures*: pg.6, Rosemary Calvert pg.19; *Still Pictures*: Gil Moti pg.32, Norbert Wu pg.41.

Cover photograph reproduced with permission of Robert Harding Picture Library.

Our thanks to Mandy Barker for her comments in the preparation of this book.

Every effort has been made to contact copyright holders of any material reproduced in this book. Any omissions will be rectified in subsequent printings if notice is given to the Publisher.

Any words appearing in the text in bold, **like this**, are explained in the Glossary.

# Contents

# What is a hurricane?

**Hurricane!** This frightening phenomenon is a wall of air that sweeps over the land, destroying everything it touches. Technically, a hurricane is a **tropical cyclone** – a fierce, inward-whirling storm with winds that rage at a speed of at least 120 kilometres per hour (75 miles per hour). The winds blow in an inward spiral from an area of **high air pressure** to an area of **low air pressure**.

# Where do hurricanes happen?

Hurricane-force winds can happen anywhere in the world, but true hurricanes are tropical storms. They blow up mostly in the tropics over the mid-Atlantic and Pacific Oceans. They hit the Caribbean Islands and the coast of the United States on one side of the world, and the Indian **subcontinent**, Japan the Far East and Northern Australia on the other.

## Hurricane highlights

The technical name for a hurricane is a tropical cyclone. There are other names, too, which come from the languages of people who live in hurricane disaster zones in different parts of the world.

Hurricane is the name given to tropical cyclones that hit the Caribbean Islands, the coast of Central America and the east coast of the United States. The word was first used by the original Native American inhabitants of the Caribbean Islands.

**Typhoon** is the name for tropical cyclones that hit China, Japan and other lands in the China Sea and the western Pacific.

Tropical cyclone is the name used for these fierce rotating storms when they affect the Indian subcontinent and Australia.

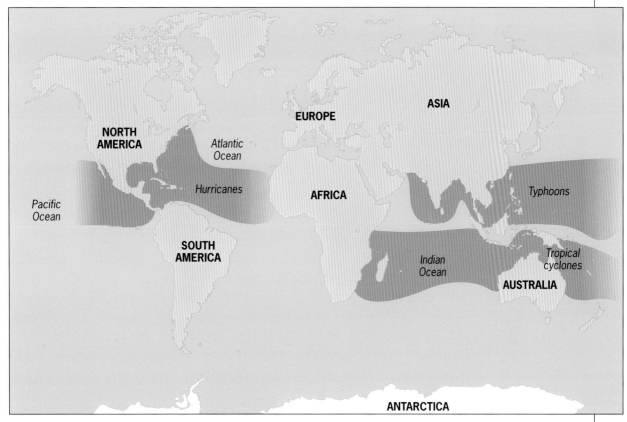

This map shows the main hurricane zones.

# Hurricanes in our hands

The strength and frequency of hurricanes seem to have increased in the last 30 years. This is thought to be due to **global warming** and the **El Niño** effect (see pages 18-21). There are differing views on the cause of these 'natural' changes, but it is believed that humans have contributed to both global warming and the El Niño effect. When fuels such as coal, oil and gas are burnt they create **carbon gases**, which rise into the atmosphere and damage it.

# Hurricanes on our minds

Have hurricanes themselves really become worse or do we just hear a lot more about them? Through satellite communications, TV and newspapers, homes throughout the world can see and listen to the devastation caused by natural disasters.

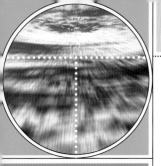

# The trail of Hurricane Georges

## Tracking Georges

The first hint of a **hurricane** on the Atlantic coast of the US begins right across the ocean in West Africa. It was here, on 13 September 1998, that a satellite image picked up the beginnings of a storm system. As warm, damp air met with cold air above, the moisture condensed and formed towering clouds.

On 15 September, ships in the area noted the first signs that a hurricane was forming. An area of very **low pressure** with winds rushing into it was observed south of the Cape Verde Islands. On 16 September the cloud and wind system became a tropical storm – the beginnings of a hurricane. For ten days it swept across the ocean, along a well-worn north-westerly track towards the Caribbean Islands. By the afternoon of 19 September, US Air Force Reserve aircraft were measuring the winds and the central air pressure of the system. Satellite information confirmed that the hurricane was getting stronger. Later that day a hurricane with strength of Force 4 on the **Saffir-Simpson hurricane scale** (see page 22) was measured. By 20 September, east of the Lesser Antilles Islands, the hurricane reached its peak.

To the north of the equator, hurricane winds blow into the central 'hole' called an eye, in an anticlockwise direction. To the south of the equator they blow in a clockwise direction.

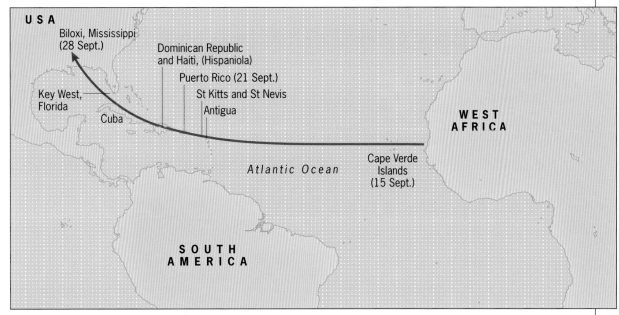

The map charts the track of Hurricane
Georges, in September 1998.

# Landfall!

Hurricane **landfall** – where the hurricane hits land –
occurred first on the island of Antigua. When the
hurricane hit the Dominican Republic and Haiti, the
cloud rose over the mountains and cooled. The **water
vapour** in it **condensed** into droplets which fell as
torrential rain. **Flash floods** and deadly mudslides
followed. From Hispaniola the hurricane moved over
Cuba and towards the United States. Here, it first hit
Key West in Florida, and slowed down as it moved
north-westward on 26–27 September. It next made
landfall on 28 September, near Biloxi in Mississippi
State, and then swirled around the southern
Mississippi, dying down all the time. By 1 October, it
was all over.

In total Hurricane Georges hit seven areas in the
Caribbean Islands and the United States between 15
September and 1 October 1998. It caused 602 deaths,
damage costing billions of dollars and a relief
programme that made a hole even in the resources of
the United States' Red Cross.

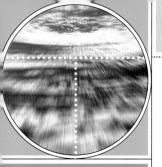

# After Hurricane Georges

Scientists are still working out the exact impact of **Hurricane** Georges. They will be examining the complicated **meteorological** and **oceanographic data** for a long time to come. Most of the data concerns the United States and the Caribbean.

## Storm surge statistics

Hurricanes cause **storm surges** as they hit the coast. Strong winds cut into the sea, helping to make a huge wall of water. Storm surges are very destructive and cause more deaths than any other hurricane feature.

So far, the height of storm surges caused by Hurricane Georges have only been estimated. On the island of Puerto Rico, they reached about 3 metres (10 feet) and on the United States mainland they reached between 1.5 and 3.7 metres (5–12 feet). Waves breaking over the top of the storm surge increased the height of the surges but this is very difficult to measure accurately.

Most **tornado** activity whips up as a hurricane moves inland. Hurricane Georges was accompanied by 28 tornadoes, mostly in Alabama and Florida, although two struck in Puerto Rico.

# Rain and flood

One of the worst features of Hurricane Georges was torrential rainfall. Over two days, Puerto Rico received 625 millimetres (25 inches), while 753 millimetres (30 inches) fell on Bay Minette in Alabama. Southern Mississippi State faced flood disaster from 30 September to 2 October, when floodwaters forced many people to **evacuate** their homes.

# Counting the cost

It is estimated that on Puerto Rico 72 605 homes were damaged, with 28 005 completely destroyed. On the island of Hispaniola, the Dominican Republic was left with 185 000 people homeless and on the other half of the island, in Haiti, 167 332 lost their homes. Many of them remained in temporary housing for several weeks as electricity and water supplies were restored. But on the mainland of the United States, Florida received damage to only 1536 homes, 173 of which were completely destroyed – mostly mobile homes (trailers). On pages 34–37 we shall see why there is such a difference between storm damage in rich and poor nations.

**Flash flooding** and mudslides on the hillsides of the Dominican Republic and Haiti caused most of the deaths in this particular hurricane disaster.

The American Red Cross mounted a huge relief operation in the United States and its islands. It became the most expensive in the organization's 117-year history. In all, the cost of Hurricane Georges has so far been estimated at £3.7 billion (US$5.9 billion).

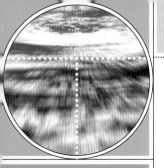

# Hitting the headlines

**Hurricane** Georges soon hit the headlines in the United States and throughout the world. National newspapers, television and radio news bulletins give a lot of important information in the days when a hurricane is approaching. These media can reach millions of people in the affected areas, who are anxiously waiting for an overall picture of what could happen. National and local Internet websites can track a hurricane on a daily and even hourly basis, giving detailed up-to-date weather information, **evacuation** instructions and advice to people living in the path.

## Rich and poor

The United States has **invested** a lot of money in modern hurricane tracking systems, and evacuation programmes. Since none of these are any use unless ordinary people can get to information, much of it is published on the Internet. Weather stations have linked up with radio and television newsrooms, which interrupt programmes if a hurricane is on the way.

The first detailed reports of hurricane disasters in developing countries usually come after the event, when foreign aid agencies and reporters start moving in to assess the damage. Compare this to the huge amount of information that is given out if a similar disaster occurs in a richer country.

Power lines are snapped, bridges are broken and roads are blocked. This means that news coverage of hurricanes is made even more difficult. Journalists who cannot get to the disaster zone can only report government statistics and information issued by aid agencies.

# Too much news?

There is more news coverage on hurricanes than ever before, with increasingly detailed accounts of the tracks they take and the traumas they cause. Does this mean that there are more hurricanes than ever before? Or does it mean that with modern technology we are able to monitor them in more detail and broadcast their effects over a wider area? All this information might lead us to believe that the world's climatic disasters are taking a turn for the worse. This affects the way we look at the impact of **global warming** and **El Niño** on hurricane disasters (see page 18–21).

**Meteorologists** at the US National Hurricane Centre monitor storm movement and development. They use satellite and **radar** information to track hurricanes, and to prepare **hurricane warnings**.

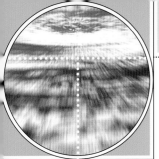

# The hurricane zones

The map on page 5 shows that the **hurricane** zones are in the hottest part of the world. This is where the heat from the Sun beats down almost directly over the equator and the tropics.

Britain is not usually on the path of true hurricanes, but the islands do occasionally suffer when an Atlantic hurricane turns northward.

The heat absorbed by the land or sea at any place in the world depends on the angle at which the Sun's rays reach the Earth at that point. This gives the Earth its different climatic zones. At the equator, where the Sun's heat beats down from directly overhead, the climate is hotter. Towards the poles, the Sun's heat hits the Earth at an angle and this leads to a cooler climate. The strong heating effect around the equator is the main reason for the movement of air masses around the Earth. The warm, **equatorial** air rises up to the **tropopause**, where the air is thinner and colder, and air from surrounding areas comes in to replace it. Having risen to the high point, air masses disperse, making their way towards the poles, where they help to create weather systems.

# Where and when?

Hurricane zones lie in the tropics, where the sea is warm – especially when the Sun is directly overhead. Then, the temperature rarely falls below 26° Celcius (79° Fahrenheit). Warm, moist air rises from the warm sea, often leading to a hurricane.

The map on page 5 shows that the largest hurricane zones are on the western sides of oceans. Deep layers of warm, moist air collect there and they fuel the hurricanes as they move westward.

Many hurricanes begin as waves of air coming from the east high up in the **Intertropical Convergence Zone**, which lies around the equator. Air is greatly heated, rises, is dispersed, then gets pulled back towards the equator again – helped by the Earth's spin. This circular movement often contributes to the start of a tropical storm system or a hurricane.

Not all hurricanes happen on the west coasts of the oceans. Many hit the north-east and north-west coasts of the Indian **subcontinent**. These particular hurricanes, called **tropical cyclones**, are caused by a change in the **monsoon winds** which blow across the land towards the south-west in winter, but turn and blow northwards across the ocean in summer from about May to September. The warm seas often give rise to fierce cyclones which devastate the coasts of Bangladesh and northern India.

In Australia, in 1974, **flash floods** were so bad that the northern city of Darwin was **evacuated**. Water rose to the tops of telegraph poles. Hundreds of thousands of sheep drowned on the flooded pastures.

# The rain and the wind

Rain is a feature of **hurricanes**, and sometimes it is torrential, causing heavy flooding. It is part of the **water cycle**. This describes the way in which the Earth's supply of water is recycled all the time in different forms. Sometimes it is held in the air as invisible **water vapour** or as tiny droplets in cloud. Sometimes it falls as rain, sleet, snow or hail. But most of it lies in massive oceans, seas, lakes and rivers, or it is frozen in ice-sheets and glaciers. The water cycle is a global system in which weather features such as rainfall can develop quickly. This makes them difficult to predict.

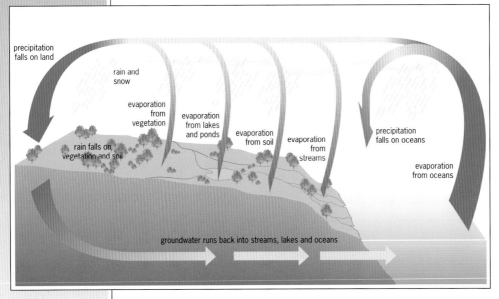

precipitation falls on land

rain and snow

evaporation from vegetation

evaporation from lakes and ponds

evaporation from soil

evaporation from streams

precipitation falls on oceans

evaporation from oceans

rain falls on vegetation and soil

groundwater runs back into streams, lakes and oceans

The amount of cloud that forms depends partly on how much moisture is **evaporated** into the air by the heat of the Sun.

# Why does the rain fall?

When the Sun shines and the wind blows over the oceans and other large water masses, it heats the water so much that some evaporates. If the air above the water is warm it holds a lot of vapour, as warm air can hold more moisture than cold air. Also warm air is less dense, or heavy, than cold air because heat makes the **molecules** move further apart. So the warm air rises, carrying the water vapour with it. As the warm, moist air rises it cools and **condenses** into tiny droplets which form clouds.

As the clouds grow even higher the super-cooled, icy droplets become larger and heavier as even more water vapour condenses. Eventually these droplets are too heavy to stay in the cloud, so they fall as rain. Some rain falls on the oceans, but a lot falls on land. Clouds rise up hill and mountain slopes, cooling and shedding rain before they reach the other side. The drops fall down the slope, gathering in tiny streams. The streams flow into rivers, and the rivers into seas. And so the cycle begins all over again.

## What makes the wind blow?

Wind is caused by air moving from areas of **high pressure** (masses of cool, dense air) to areas of **low pressure** (masses of rising, warm air). This exchange of air masses can be quite gentle – just a faint breeze might blow. But if there is an area of very low pressure, caused by a lot of warm air rising, then air from the high pressure area rushes in fast, in the form of winds, to fill the space. This rush of wind is what makes a hurricane so strong.

This is dark, towering, **cumulonimbus** cloud. It is this type of cloud that can develop into a hurricane as it sweeps across warm sea. **Tornadoes**, too, come from this type of cloud – from bulges that hang down at the bottom.

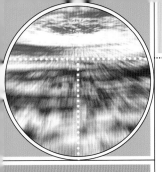

# How do hurricanes happen?

## Under pressure

**Hurricanes** develop where winds meet in the tropics, usually in summer and autumn – between mid-May and November. Hurricanes form as great masses of very warm and very moist air rise. The rising air causes areas of very **low air pressure** which form the centre around which the warm air rises in a whirling, upward spiral. As it does so, cooler air from an area of **high pressure** rushes into the space it has left at its base.

The rising air cools as it goes up. The moisture in the air **condenses**, forming banks of very heavy, lowlying, rain-bearing cloud. The continual formation of cloud and the rolling thunderstorms also releases heat into the air, which fuels the whirling hurricane even more. The upward-turning spiral and the downward-rushing air move faster and faster as they approach land, and the sea provides very little resistance to it. Once the hurricane begins to move over the land, there is no more warm moisture to pick up, so the 'fuel' begins to run out. There is also more friction with land and vegetation than there is with water. This friction slows the wind and the hurricane gradually dies, but the damage has already been done.

**The map shows that the main (prevailing) winds in the tropics curl towards the equator.**

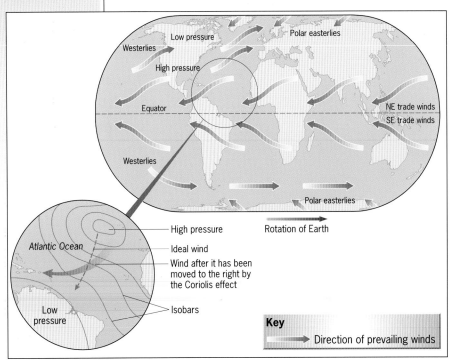

Low pressure

Westerlies

High pressure

Polar easterlies

Equator

NE trade winds

SE trade winds

Westerlies

Polar easterlies

Rotation of Earth

Atlantic Ocean

High pressure

Ideal wind

Wind after it has been moved to the right by the Coriolis effect

Low pressure

Isobars

**Key**

Direction of prevailing winds

# What helps the hurricane spin?

If air moved in a simple, straight direction from high pressure to low pressure then hurricanes might not happen at all. As the Earth spins from west to east, air movement is shifted slightly. North of the equator it moves to the right, and to the south it moves to the left. This is caused by the **Coriolis force**. Although it is less powerful at the tropics and the equator than at the poles, it still causes the hurricane to turn.

# The eye of the storm

The eye is formed when a hurricane reaches its peak. It is a wide column of calm, descending air right in the middle of the cylinder of warm, rising air that is wrapped around it. This tube of dry air, surrounded by walls of cloud, reaches up to a clear, blue, sunny sky.

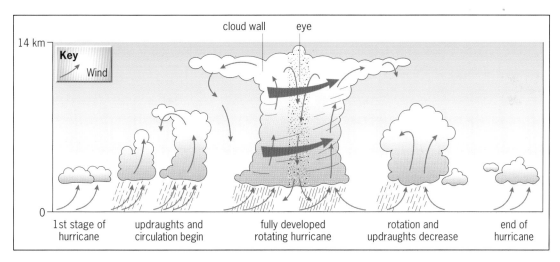

When the hurricane begins to develop, the contrasts in temperatures and air pressure within the hurricane help to increase its power. As the eye grows, it allows more of the Sun's energy to heat up the sea, which creates more moisture in the air, and a big contrast in temperature with the cooler outside wall of the hurricane.

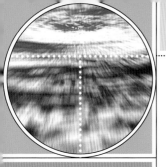

# The effects of El Niño – making things worse?

In recent years **El Niño** has been the most talked-about cause of freak natural disasters in the world. This phenomenon creates great extremes, from violent **hurricanes** and terrifying twisters, torrential rain and heavy flooding to severe drought, dust storms and forest fires. It also makes predicting and coping with the natural disasters almost impossible. There is thought to be a similar phenomenon in the atmosphere above the Atlantic. This change in **air pressure** and winds is known as the North Atlantic Oscillation (NAO). It affects western Europe and North Africa.

The phenomenon was first noticed by anchovy fishermen off the coast of Peru. Every few years the cold coastal waters and the air above them warmed up, causing more moisture to be **evaporated** into the air. This brought welcome rain to the dry shores of Peru around Christmas time. Over the years, however, this mild, welcomed climatic variation has brought a series of dreaded disasters.

## The power of El Niño

El Niño is a very strange and complex climatic feature, affecting both the northern and southern **hemispheres** of the Earth – and the two largest oceans. It begins in the Pacific Ocean as a sudden reversal of the prevailing winds, which normally blow in a predictable east-west direction all year round (see the diagram on page 16). These changing winds blow towards the coast of South America, warming up the water and the air as they go. As we saw on pages 16–17, a combination of warm water and air can create storm clouds and violent hurricane-force winds.

Neither of these dramatic changes in the atmosphere acts on its own. It is believed that changes in the oceans' powerful currents affect the weather patterns above. Scientists now also believe that **global warming** plays a part in El Niño.

We can discover a lot about El Niños and climates of the past by studying tree rings. Each ring in a tree's trunk represents one year's growth. When the ring is narrow it means that the tree has not grown very fast. It has either not had enough moisture or enough sunlight. We can also look at soil sediments at the bottom of the ocean, thick ice at the poles and coral reefs.

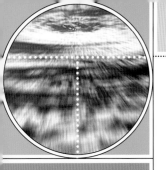

# Global warming – and more hurricanes?

Most scientists agree that the world's climate is getting warmer. Scientists are sure that it takes a difference of only 1-2° Celsius (1.8-3.6° Fahrenheit) to change the Earth's climate and weather patterns quite dramatically. It is thought that in 30 years' time the Earth will be at least 1° Celsius (1.8° Fahrenheit ) hotter.

## Living in a greenhouse

The **greenhouse effect** is thought to be partly responsible for **global warming**. It is caused by **carbon gases**, particularly carbon dioxide, rising into the atmosphere. Heat from the Sun is absorbed by the Earth and some is reflected and **radiated** back. These gases form a layer which acts like a huge mirror, reflecting this radiated heat back down to Earth and warming both the sea and the land.

About 80 per cent of carbon gases are produced by burning fossil fuels such as coal and oil in power stations, factories and homes throughout the world. But the greenhouse effect is not thought to be acting on its own in increasing climatic change.

As the Earth warms up even more ice will melt at the poles, as will frozen tundra lands, such as those of Siberia in Russia, shown in the picture. This will release **methane** gases from decayed plant matter trapped underneath the ice and increase the greenhouse effect even more.

# A hole in the sky

The Earth is surrounded by layers of gases known as the atmosphere. It stops the full strength of the Sun from reaching the Earth and filters harmful **ultra-violet rays**. One of the most effective protective gases is **ozone**, which forms a layer in the **stratosphere**, between 10 and 50 kilometres (about 6–30 miles) above the Earth. In recent years, the layer of ozone has thinned, especially over Antarctica. This has led, among other things, to increased **radiation** from the Sun.

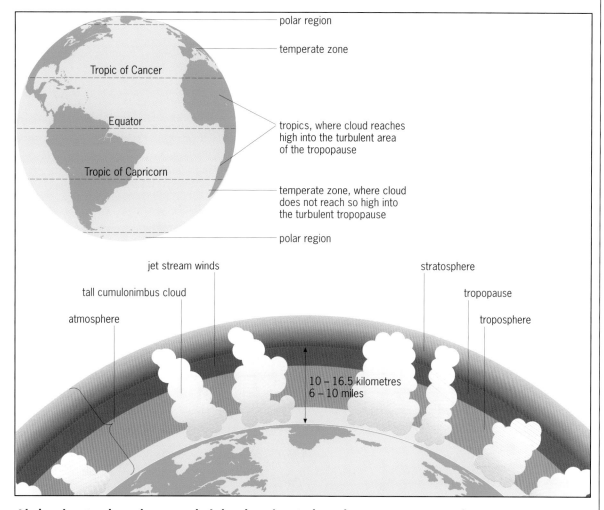

polar region

temperate zone

Tropic of Cancer

Equator

Tropic of Capricorn

tropics, where cloud reaches high into the turbulent area of the tropopause

temperate zone, where cloud does not reach so high into the turbulent tropopause

polar region

jet stream winds

tall cumulonimbus cloud

atmosphere

stratosphere

tropopause

troposphere

10 – 16.5 kilometres
6 – 10 miles

Air begins to slow down and sink when it reaches the **tropopause** – the layer between the **troposphere** and the stratosphere. There is more **turbulence** in the tropical tropopause than in other parts of the layer. This is why weather phenomena such as **hurricanes** and **tornado**es occur so often on either side of the equator.

**21**

# Wind, rain, flood and mud

What happens when a **hurricane** hits land? There are three main destructive forces: raging wind, torrential rain and sliding mud. Together they kill humans and animals, they destroy buildings, bridges, roads and railways, and devastate crops. The most obvious cause is the wind, which can snap mature trees in half and even bend and break steel structures. The table below shows what happens when hurricanes of different forces hit the land. It is known as the **Saffir-Simpson hurricane scale**.

| Status | Wind strength (knots) | Wind strength (mph) | Damage potential |
|---|---|---|---|
| Depression | up to 35 | up to 38 | |
| Tropical storm | 35–64 | 38–73 | |
| Category 1 Hurricane | 65–83 | 74–95 | Flooding of lowlying areas, flying debris and fallen trees. Homes not tied down suffer the most damage, especially mobile homes. Fishing piers may suffer damage. |
| Category 2 Hurricane | 84–95 | 96–110 | There is significant damage to mobile homes, vegetation and piers. There is a little damage to doors, roofing materials and windows on buildings. |
| Category 3 Hurricane | 96–113 | 111–130 | Mobile homes are destroyed. Some damage to homes and buildings. Coastal homes and buildings are flooded. |
| Category 4 Hurricane | 114–134 | 131–155 | Homes and buildings are severely damaged or destroyed. Major flooding occurs along the coastline and inland. |
| Category 5 Hurricane | 135 or more | 156 or more | Homes and buildings are completely destroyed. Severe flooding occurs well inland. |

# Flowing mud

On bare slopes, torrential rain combines with loose earth and gravel to form a heavy mass of mud, which slides to the bottom of the slope by the action of gravity. Mudslides are common features when hurricanes hit areas where there has been large-scale deforestation or tree-felling.

# Fear of flood

Flooding can be the most dangerous result of hurricane forces. This is especially so in large **delta** areas such as the coast of Bangladesh, where the Brahmaputra, Ganges and Jahmuna rivers meet the sea. Rain sweeps inland with the **tropical cyclone** and swells the rivers so the flow of water through the **floodplain** and coastal delta are greatly increased. Then coming towards them from the sea is a great wall of water – a hurricane **storm surge**! Flooding also occurs further inland, as the hurricane winds drive the clouds away from the sea towards cooler, drier air.

In 1996, Hurricane Fran hit the US capital city of Washington and the surrounding area. In just a few hours, 102 millimetres (4 inches) lashed down on the city streets. This picture from Alexandria, Virginia shows the scale of the problem.

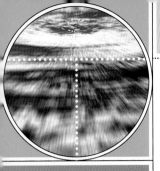

# Walls of water

A **storm surge** is the most feared outcome of a **hurricane**, especially in the western Pacific and along the lowlying coasts of Bangladesh, Pakistan and north-west India. A storm surge is created when strong winds cut into the sea, helping to make a huge wall of water that rises and drives towards the shore.

Some waves can reach a height of 8 metres (30 feet) causing severe coastal flooding. This is made worse by a general rise in sea level of up to 50 centimetres (20 inches).

Torrential rain on the sea and the coast, and a high tide can make the situation even worse. It is very difficult to know how many deaths a storm surge on its own causes, but it is estimated that about 90 per cent of deaths along a flooded coast are caused by drowning in these huge waves. It is believed that because of **global warming**, the sea level has risen about 15 centimetres (6 inches) over the last 100 years – and it's still rising, making flooding more likely.

## Hurricane highlights

The level of the storm surge depends on:

- the speed of the storm's forward motion
- the distance from the storm centre to the eye wall
- the **air pressure** at the centre of the eye – the lower it is, the faster the wind but also the more seawater will get sucked up
- the steepness of the sea floor as it rises to the coast – and therefore the normal depths of water close to the shore
- the shape of the seafloor as it rises to the coast
- the angle of the storm as it hits the coast.

This picture shows the polder lands of the Netherlands – vast areas of farmland reclaimed from the sea. In February 1953 a massive storm surge caused by hurricane-force winds flooded the polders, most of which are at, or below, sea level. Nearly 2000 people were drowned, 72 000 were evacuated from their homes and about 50 000 cattle died.

# Storm surge stories

In 1938, 600 people were swept to their death by a storm surge as a hurricane hit Rhode Island in the United States. A wall of water 4.3 metres (14 feet) high swept through the streets. Nowadays, earlier warnings can be given so that the islanders have time to **evacuate**. Over the years, the population has increased so much that the death toll would be even worse if there was no time to escape.

In 1969, Hurricane Camille battered the coasts of Florida and Mississippi. An 8.2-metre (27-foot) storm surge drowned 300 people who could not get out of the way in time.

As well as causing huge loss of life, storm surges are devastating in other ways. Sand is swept inland, covering coastal roads and **sandblasting** buildings. Harbour walls, roads and bridges connecting islands are broken. The salt water rots wooden structures and pollutes farmland.

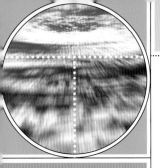

# On the edge of the hurricane – tornadoes

Many **hurricanes** are made worse by violent, twisting, sucking winds that often whirl alongside them, mostly over land. These are known as **tornadoes** or twisters – fast winds that rotate around a funnel of very **low pressure**. They form inside deep **cumulonimbus** thunderclouds, and appear to hang from them in an upside-down cone.

The funnel may be quite narrow – no more than 100 metres (330 feet) across at its widest point – or it may be as much as 1.5 kilometres (about 1 mile). The tornado's path may be as short as a few kilometres (1–2 miles) or it might run for 750 kilometres (466 miles)!

The United States suffers more tornadoes than any other country in the world – often 1000 or more in a year. The area of the United States most commonly hit by tornadoes has been called **Tornado Alley**. It runs from the Gulf of Mexico, through Oklahoma and Kansas, right up to the Great Lakes. Australia, Canada, parts of Russia, central Asia, Japan, Italy and even the UK are also tornado targets.

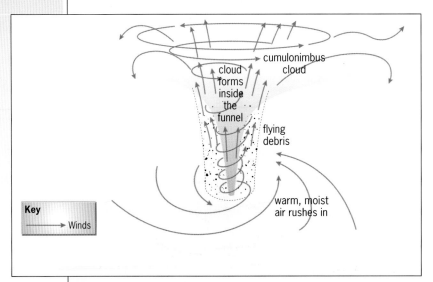

cumulonimbus cloud

cloud forms inside the funnel

flying debris

warm, moist air rushes in

Key
⟶ Winds

This shows how the tornado spins and the conditions it needs to keep going, but no one knows exactly what makes the spin begin.

# How do tornadoes form?

Tornadoes often run in clusters to the right of incoming hurricanes, but they build up mostly over land, not over the sea. They need some of the same conditions as hurricanes in order to form and maintain their spin. They begin in an area of very low pressure and they need a layer of very warm, humid air near the ground which rises to meet a mass of cool, dry air very high above.

A horizontal wind blows continually at an angle caused by the **Coriolis force**, and the twisting motion begins. Air rushes in at the bottom, to replace the warm, rising air, sucking air up faster through the funnel as it does so. Thunderclouds form inside the funnel as the lowest layer keeps warming up. They **condense** quite low down and release more heat, fuelling the tornado.

# Tracking the tornado

For over 20 years, tornadoes have been quite successfully tracked by scientists using the **Doppler radar** system. The radar picks up electrical signals inside a thunderstorm and can detect when a circular movement of wind is about to move out of it. Radar is especially important for tracking tornadoes that cannot easily be spotted – at night time or when they are wrapped in cloud or torrential rain.

When tornadoes hit the ground they suck up everything they touch – roofs, walls, cars, trees, telegraph poles and people.

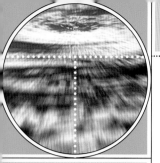

# Tracking the hurricane

The map on page 5 shows that **hurricanes** usually occur in the same parts of the world. Each year, they make their way in the usual direction along well-worn routes, but their **landfall** – the place where the hurricane hits the land – is not the same every time. Tracking the exact path and predicting landfall is therefore very important. So are assessing the width of the hurricane, the strength, the duration (the time it lasts), the height of **storm surges** and the amount and duration of rainfall.

## Hurricane highlights

Specialists from different areas of science work together to predict hurricanes. **Meteorologists** study the climate and the atmosphere. **Oceanographers** look at the change in temperature and currents of the oceans. The following are some of the things they look for:

- Warm seas that are at temperatures of at least 26° Celcius (about 79° Fahrenheit) down to a depth of 60 metres (about 200 feet) are perfect fuel for a hurricane.

- Deep, dark cloud, thunderstorms and towering **cumulonimbus** clouds, are typical signals of a hurricane and can be monitored using aircraft **radar** and satellite images.

- Hook-shaped clouds are the first definite signs that a hurricane is beginning its turning motion. As they grow and spin they are monitored by **Doppler radar** and satellite.

- Storm surges – to work out the height of a storm surge, oceanographers calculate the **air pressure** on the sea, the speed of the storm, the position of the centre of the hurricane, its size, the height of the tide and the shape of the coastline. This gives them a good idea how high the waters will rise.

# Prediction problems

Computer models of previous hurricanes help predict where, when and how fiercely the hurricane will hit land, but these can easily be inaccurate. Sometimes, a landfall can occur more than 100 kilometres (60 miles) away from the predicted spot! Problems arise when the hurricane hits islands and then continues over more sea before its final landfall on the mainland. The islands slow the hurricane down, and often alter its course, and it is difficult to predict how much speed it will pick up again before it hits the next coastline.

Hurricanes can swerve as landfall occurs. This is partly due to the Earth's spin pushing the winds off course – the **Coriolis force** – and partly due to the slowing-down of the hurricane as it reaches the land.

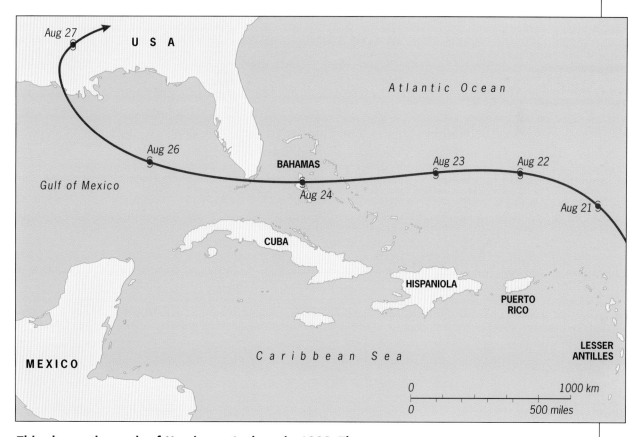

This shows the path of Hurricane Andrew in 1992. The map shows how Hurricane Andrew swerved from a north-west direction to the north-east when it hit the Florida coast.

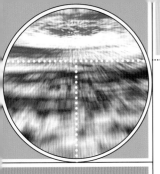

# Hunting the hurricane

**Meteorologists** use information gathered by satellite, civilian and military aircraft, ships, air balloons and coastal **radar** to monitor the **hurricane** as it makes its way across the ocean. Together these data give a detailed picture of the hurricane's size, shape, direction, turning speed, approach speed, moisture content and cloud type.

## Tracking Georges

This is just a small bite of all the information gathered and plotted every six hours as Hurricane Georges grew into a hurricane. Look up the latitude and longitude in an atlas to see where the hurricane was going. We can see from the table when the cyclone changed from a tropical depression into a tropical storm and then into hurricane. In this table, windspeed has been measured in knots, or nautical miles per hour. One knot is the same as 1.825 kilometres (1.151 miles) per hour.

| Date | Time | Latitude (north) | Longitude (west) | Pressure (**millibars**) | Windspeed (knots) | Stage |
|------|------|------------------|------------------|--------------------------|-------------------|-------|
| 09/15 | 1200 | 9.7 | 25.1 | 1009 | 30 | Tropical depression |
| 09/15 | 1800 | 9.8 | 26.5 | 1009 | 30 | Tropical depression |
| 09/16 | 0000 | 10.0 | 28.1 | 1009 | 30 | Tropical depression |
| 09/16 | 0600 | 10.3 | 29.7 | 1009 | 30 | Tropical depression |
| 09/16 | 1200 | 10.6 | 31.3 | 1005 | 35 | Tropical storm |
| 09/16 | 1800 | 11.0 | 32.9 | 1003 | 35 | Tropical storm |
| 09/17 | 0000 | 11.3 | 34.6 | 1000 | 45 | Tropical storm |
| 09/17 | 0600 | 11.7 | 36.3 | 997 | 50 | Tropical storm |
| 09/17 | 1200 | 12.0 | 38.1 | 994 | 55 | Tropical storm |
| 09/17 | 1800 | 12.3 | 40.0 | 987 | 65 | Hurricane |

This tracking table continued until the hurricane died on 1 October 1998 at 6.00 a.m.

# Hurricane hunters

In the United States, the Air Force Reserve actually fly aircraft into the eye of the hurricane! The aircraft are designed to withstand the buffeting winds and the flight crew are trained to navigate through the cloud and the **turbulence** within the hurricane. They measure flight-level windspeeds and **air pressure** at the centre of the storm.

# Getting the picture

**Doppler radar** is used to estimate the shape of a hurricane and the circulation of wind. Doppler radar sends out a radio signal which is reflected by droplets of moisture in the hurricane back to the receiver. When several Doppler radars are used, a three-dimensional picture of cloud circulation is built up. This gives an idea of windspeed and direction within the storm.

During Hurricane Georges, the US Air Force Reserve and the National Oceanic and Atmospheric Administration flew a total of 23 missions to measure windspeed and pressure in the centre of the hurricane. This hurricane spotter plane has a radome radar system in its nose.

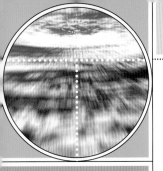

# Hurricane warning!

## A problem of timing

The prediction of **hurricanes** must be matched by good warning systems, which all countries in the tropical hurricane zones have developed. A good warning will give people 24 hours to prepare for a hurricane, although it is not easy to say exactly where a hurricane will strike so far in advance. Huge numbers of people over wide areas therefore have to be warned, just in case the hurricane strikes. In the western Pacific, hundreds of tiny islands lie in the path of hurricanes. It is even more difficult here to predict the strength of the hurricane and give people proper warning. It is impossible to **evacuate** people on a very small island, so finding protective shelter in good time is the only answer.

Many big cities lie in the path of hurricanes. Here, evacuation is an enormous, costly undertaking, growing even bigger as urban populations increase. **Meteorologists** are under a lot of pressure to find ways of predicting hurricanes more accurately. This will lead to better preparation over smaller areas, saving lives and lowering costs. It takes about £125 000 (US$200 000) to evacuate just 2.5 square kilometres (one square mile) of a residential area.

Bangladesh has very up-to-date hurricane prediction systems, but the geography of Bangladesh makes it very difficult to know exactly how badly a hurricane will affect it. Most people live on the **floodplain**, or on sandbanks called chars near the wide river **estuaries**. When rain lashes down on the river estuary water levels rise, which acts with the in-coming **storm surge** to create massive flooding.

# Getting ready – keeping in touch

On the south-east coast of the United States, the first phase of the alert begins about 24 hours before the hurricane hits. This phase is known as **'hurricane watch'**. Since it is uncertain where **landfall** will occur, there is no evacuation – people just make sure they check regularly with the radio, television news or on the Internet.

About six hours later, hurricane landfall predictions are more accurate. This is because the hurricane is approaching coastal **radar** stations, which can help to calculate statistics more precisely. From this time onwards, specific warnings, called **hurricane warnings**, are issued in danger zones. This is when people begin to carry out their local evacuation plan.

Hurricane Gilbert struck the Caribbean Island of Jamaica on 12 September 1988. It was one of the worst hurricanes in the island's history. A quarter of all the houses were badly damaged or destroyed. Parts of the airport (above) were ruined and the planes were wrecked. But only 45 people died. This is because Jamaica has well-organized and well-publicized evacuation plans.

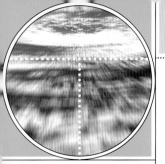

# Preventing the damage

Many **hurricane** zones take in some of the poorest countries in the world. Many people live in poor-quality housing right in the path of the winds. These homes are constructed of wood, plastic and corrugated-iron sheeting – materials that break and blow away easily. In coastal areas, **storm surges** soak wooden structures with salt water, which eventually rots the wood. Even concrete foundations and walls eventually crumble if they are submerged in salt water.

## Houses for hurricanes

Countries such as Jamaica and Australia have put strict building codes into place in hurricane zones. In Jamaica, corrugated iron roofs have to be tied down with hurricane straps. New buildings have to withstand 3-second gusts of 200 kilometres per hour (about 125 miles per hour). In Australia, buildings less than 6 metres (about 20 feet) tall have to be able to cope with winds of up to 150 kilometres per hour (about 90 miles per hour).

Hurricanes cause a lot of economic problems in poorer countries. This is partly because storm damage ruins cash crops, which are often the main or only export. Exports are goods that are sold abroad, and they bring in much-needed money.

# Plant planning

Hurricanes cause food shortages in poorer countries but it is difficult to assess crop damage immediately after the disaster. The initial impact is obvious: fruit trees and tall-stemmed crops are broken and bent and leaves are ripped off. Some plants simply topple over, their roots loosened by floodwater and torrential rain. Others are smothered in mud and debris. Other, less obvious effects only emerge after time. These include rotted root crops and fruit trees that appear to have survived but which later do not bear fruit – blossom and young fruit having been blown off in the wind. So what are the solutions?

Some of the answers are to plant specially-developed crops with shorter stems that will not break in the wind. Other solutions include planting crops that have a short growing season, so that they can be planted or harvested before the hurricane season. Planting more crops over a larger area increases the chances of a reasonable harvest, whatever the weather.

One way of not being hurt by hurricanes is to move away from the disaster zone. The new capital city of Belize now lies 80 kilometres (50 miles) inland. On 31 October 1961, the original city was flattened by Hurricane Hattie, and 2000 people were killed.

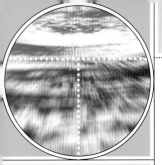

# Why live in danger?

Millions of people in different parts of the world live in the paths of **hurricanes**. This is not because they do not realize the dangers, but because they have to make a living. Some of the world's most fertile regions like Bangladesh are situated on **floodplains** near river **estuaries**. In hurricane zones, these are also areas that are badly affected by **storm surges**. Coastal ports face the same problem. Many of these, too, are situated on estuaries, where goods can be transported downriver and shipped all over the world. River water is used in the manufacturing of wood-products, chemicals, cloth and many other goods – and in the cooling-towers of power stations. Many people enjoy living on the coast with its beautiful scenery and fresh sea air.

The islands of Japan face **typhoons** from the western Pacific Ocean. These hit the eastern shores of Japan where the country's largest cities are. This is because of the warm ocean current that runs along the coast. Warm waters fuel the hurricanes but, for the islanders, they also provide a better climate for agriculture. This, plus fishing, are what first attracted people to the east coast, where great cities have developed.

# Cities at risk

Cities attract workers, and in much of the developing world huge numbers of poor farmers migrate to them to find wage-earning jobs. They build their homes on the edges, often on surrounding hillsides where there is a threat of mudslides. The houses are often makeshift and there are often no rules governing how they are constructed. **Sanitation** is poor. So in hurricane-prone cities in the developing world, a hurricane disaster causes a large loss of life and a lot of storm damage. Poor sanitation leads to a huge health hazard.

In all inner city areas, space is very limited so buildings have to be tall. In hurricane zones, new high-rise constructions have to comply with strict building regulations. These control construction methods and materials used for foundations, frames and walls. Older buildings are very vulnerable to storm damage. Two kinds of hurricane wind threaten the city – a swirling **vortex** of winds bouncing around tall buildings, and the **Venturi effect**, where windspeed increases as it is channelled through narrow streets lined with high-rise buildings.

In the United States, a lot of damage occurs in residential areas on the edges of cities. Newer block-built houses usually suffer a small amount of structural damage, but many people are housed in trailer parks, with lightweight trailers (residential caravans) that are easily blown over by the winds.

Beautiful beaches and hot, sunny weather have attracted millions of tourists to Miami Beach in Florida, which is right in the path of hurricanes.

# Hurricanes in history

**Hurricanes** have been around for a long time, as shown by stories of ancient storms. We know that weather conditions in small areas were recorded as long ago as the fourteenth century. Death tolls in the United States and Caribbean have been counted for over 300 years. But it is only in the last 100 years or so that governments and authorities have tried to assess the damage through pictures and eyewitness accounts.

It is only in the last 100 years, too, that we have tried to look at the causes of hurricanes in a methodical, scientific way. **Barometers** used for measuring **air pressure** have been around for centuries. So too have weather vanes for locating the direction of the wind. But meteorology itself – the study of climate and the atmosphere – came into being a mere 80 years ago, after World War One. Tracking hurricanes using satellite images has only been made possible in the last 20 years – a short time in scientific terms.

In Texas, USA, the city of Galveston was savagely hit by a hurricane in 1900. Over 12 000 people are thought to have died – most drowned by a **storm surge**. It was the first disaster ever filmed, and it was shot by the famous inventor of the lightbulb, Thomas Edison.

# Historical hurricanes

The list on page 44 shows the ten most deadly hurricanes recorded, but we do not know if they were the ten most deadly hurricanes ever. Modern meteorology has allowed us to predict how often the worst hurricanes are likely to occur. From this we can work back in time and estimate what the damage might have been to communities of the past. One of the calculations made by modern **meteorologists** is that the worst hurricanes – Force 5 – occur roughly only once every 100 years. But this calculation was thrown out when Hurricane Gilbert hit the Caribbean Islands, Mexico and Texas in 1988, and Hurricane Andrew fell on southern Florida in 1992. Both were Force 5 storms. Does this mean that there have been more severe hurricanes in history than we thought?

Hurricane-force winds, although not strictly a true hurricane, hit Britain in 1703. At least 100 people were killed on land but it is thought that 8000 probably perished at sea. This tells us that there were many more fishermen and trading ships than there are today. Cities were much smaller and only increased during the industrial revolution that began about 80 years later. Throughout the world at this time, populations were smaller and more spread-out, so hurricane death tolls would probably not have been as great as they have been in the last 200 years.

Over 200 years ago, a hurricane hit the Lesser Antilles Islands in the Caribbean. Over 20 000 people died, making it the sixth worst hurricane in recorded history.

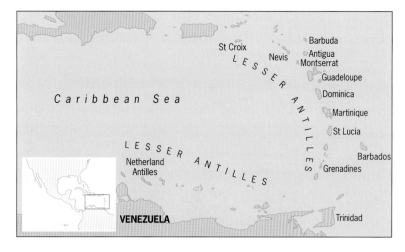

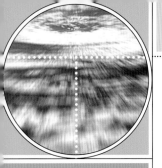

# Taking advantage – the natural world

When **hurricanes** hit farmlands, cultivated plants bend, break or rot in the soil. It is a similar story with farm animals. Animals in the wild might be able to sense a storm coming and be able to get out of the way. On a farm, though, they are often penned in with nowhere to go. Have plants and animals in the natural world adapted any better to hurricanes?

Along the west Atlantic coast one of the first signs of a hurricane coming are flocks of frigate birds swooping inland.

## Warnings in West Africa

A type of hurricane is very frequent in West Africa, just as the rainy season begins. We hear very little about them because they rarely cause loss of life, but they certainly damage buildings and destroy crops and livestock. Basically, the very warm, moist air from the Atlantic creates an area of **low pressure** that moves inland, towards the Sahara. Here, the climate is extremely hot and dry, creating a huge **high pressure** area which blows southward into the area of low pressure. The hurricanes created by this **turbulence** affect the normally very dry Sahel and savannah regions. Here, natural plants have adapted to hurricane conditions. Tight clumps of grasses and short trees have strong spreading roots that cling tightly to the soil. Grass blades and shrubs sway in a rotating motion so they do not snap easily.

Creatures, too, have developed ways of surviving and even taking advantage of hurricanes. Quelea birds (say, 'kwelya') are a kind of weaver bird, which weave colonies of rounded, protective nests attached to tree branches. Dozens of nests cling to the tree and sway unharmed with the branches as the wind rages.

Locusts take advantage of the storms. Locust eggs are laid in the newly-wet soil, dampened by the rains that precede the storms. The eggs hatch in the warm, humid days that follow, then swarms of them are transported by hurricanes to feeding grounds all over West and North Africa. Here, the farmer loses out again, for the locusts eat everything green in sight – and even clothes hung out to dry!

Coral animals that build the reefs that protect the American coastlands **spawn** – or lay eggs – just before the onset of the hurricane season. These eggs float around the reef until the hurricane **storm surge** arrives, and the swaying seas transport the coral eggs over a wide area, where they begin life afresh.

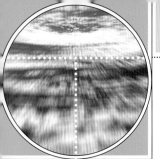

# The storm is coming

Rainforest birds on the Caribbean Islands build their weatherproof nests among the tall, wide trees, which create a huge protective canopy over the forest floor. The trees are anchored well into the ground with massive, twisted root systems, so when the **hurricane** winds hit them they stand their ground. Leaves and twigs are ripped from branches, which bend or snap depending on how flexible they are. By this time, the birds have abandoned their nests and found cover on the forest floor. The heavy rains now reach through the broken canopy down onto the thin soil. The ground is soaked and the roots of the weakest rainforest trees loosen. Terrific winds are still blowing and some trees finally fall. Some of the birds are lucky – their nests are left intact on the strongest trees. Others will quickly have to rebuild their nests before the mating season ends. But is it all bad news for the natural world?

Amphibians, such as frogs and lizards, are very sensitive to the sudden, deep drop in **air pressure** as the hurricane approaches. They call out for hours at time until the hurricane arrives.

# Winners and losers

Rainforest insects are now exposed to the light by the broken canopy and are eaten gratefully by hungry birds. But the humming-bird, which feeds on nectar, has to search hard for blossoms on the fallen trees. Thin-skinned amphibians are now exposed to the shrivelling sun. But the fallen, broken tree trunks have provided pools of water for frogs to lay their eggs in.

These seabirds are taking advantage of extra fish and seafood brought to the surface by the hurricane.

After a few days, the humid air and the moist earth give just the right conditions for new trees to grow – especially species that get only a rare chance to push up between the thick trunks of the largest rainforest trees. Thinner-trunked trees such as the trumpet tree find their place in the forest.

As the hurricane moves over the east coast of the United States, different habitats are hit. In the pine forests, the woodpecker surveys the brittle, fallen trunk of a long-leaved pine tree, where it had spent two years building its home. Now it will have to start all over again. But in the marshlands hit by a huge **storm surge**, the alligator is happy. Its hard, earth nest lies untouched by the storm.

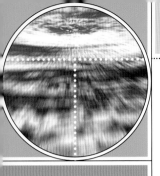

# Amazing hurricanes

## The ten most deadly hurricanes in history

| Place | Year | Number of deaths |
|---|---|---|
| Bangladesh | 1970 | Up to 500 000 |
| Bangladesh | 1991 | 131 000 |
| South-east India | 1977 | 100 000 |
| Bangladesh | 1964 | 35 000 |
| North-east India and Bangladesh | 1965 | 30 000 |
| Lesser Antilles (Caribbean Sea) | 1780 | 22 000 |
| Bangladesh | 1963 | 15 000 |
| Bangladesh | 1964 | 15 000 |
| Texas, USA | 1900 | 12 000 |
| Bangladesh | 1985 | 11 000 |

## Breaking the bank

These are the five most costly **hurricanes** so far for the United States. The cost of Hurricane Georges is still being counted. Hurricanes cause more damage than any other natural disaster.

| Date | Hurricane | Cost in billions of pounds | Cost in billions of US dollars |
|---|---|---|---|
| 1992 | Andrew | 9.7 | 15.5 |
| 1989 | Hugo | 2.6 | 4.2 |
| 1992 | Iniki | 1.0 | 1.6 |
| 1979 | Frederic | 0.47 | 0.75 |
| 1983 | Alicia | 0.43 | 0.68 |

# The biggest weapon

Many of the deaths in the table opposite were caused by **storm surges**, the worst of which occur on the Indian **subcontinent**, especially in the north around the Bay of Bengal, where **tropical cyclones** happen almost every year. Lowlying, highly-populated islands add to their impact. One of the deadliest storm surges in history hit the area south-west of Calcutta, in India in 1876. On its own, it is believed to have killed 100 000 people.

# Naming hurricanes

Hurricanes are always given names – such as Hurricane Andrew or Hurricane Georges. This started over 100 years ago when an Australian **meteorologist** called Clement Wragge began identifying the storms using characters from mythology. He then moved on to politicians' names, which is when his system collapsed – the politicians did not like it! But the method of identification was renewed about 60 years ago and became the official system in 1952. At the beginning of the year, the first hurricane is given a name beginning with 'A', the next, 'B' and so on. They are given alternating male and female names.

The Netherlands were hit by a huge storm surge caused by hurricane force winds on 31 January 1953. Floods swept 65 kilometres (40 miles) inland and 3000 people died. The disaster was so severe because a lot of the land lay below sea level. Since then, huge steel and concrete barriers have been built to keep out the waves. The one in the picture, at Neelje Jans, is also a park.

# Glossary

**air pressure**   the amount of pressure put on the sea or land by the air – high pressure areas have cold, dense, descending air, while low pressure areas have warm, lighter, rising air

**barometer**   instrument for measuring air pressure

**carbon gases**   gases formed by burning fossil fuels such as coal and oil

**condense**   when water vapour is cooled enough for water droplets to form

**Coriolis force**   the effect of the Earth's spin on winds – curving them towards the right to the north of the equator, and to the left to the south of the equator

**cumulonimbus (cloud)**   heavy, rain-bearing thundercloud

**delta**   the mouth of a river – where the river meets the sea

**Doppler radar**   radio waves reflected off super-cooled water droplets or ice particles in thunderclouds show the movement inside the cloud; it can reveal the hook-shape of a forming tornado

**easterly jet**   a surge of cold wind high up and from the east – at about 10 000 metres (about 30 000 feet) above the Earth

**El Niño**   the effect of changing wind directions and warm ocean currents on the climate, and on climatic features such as hurricanes and tornadoes

**equatorial**   around the equator (usually refers to climate)

**estuary**   very lowlying wet area where a river meets the sea

**evacuate**   to leave an area that is about to experience a disaster

**evaporate**   when liquid changes into a gas or vapour

**flash flood**   a sudden flood caused by torrential rainfall

**floodplain**   the low, flat area of land around where a river widens

**front**   the zone where high pressure areas and low pressure areas meet

**global warming**   a rise in temperature around the Earth – possibly due to the emission of carbon gases into the air, possibly due to flares from the Sun

**greenhouse effect**   when carbon gases released into the atmosphere reflect heat back onto the Earth

**hemisphere**   the halves of the world north and south of the equator

**high pressure**   large areas of cool, dense air that sink into areas of low pressure

**hurricane**   an inward-whirling wind raging at least 120 kilometres per hour (75 miles per hour) – this is the name used on the Caribbean Islands, Central America and the East coast of the United States (see also tropical cyclone, and typhoon)

**hurricane warning**   a late phase of hurricane warning when evacuation plans are carried out

**hurricane watch**   an early phase of hurricane warning on the east coast of the United States

**Intertropical Convergence Zone (ITCZ)**   the area around the equator where air is heated, rises, is dispersed and then gets pulled back down towards the Earth again

**invested**   to put money into a project

**landfall**   when a hurricane hits land

**low pressure**   large areas of warm, rising and often moist air that are often stopped in their tracks by areas of high air pressure

**meteorological data**   facts and figures relating to the weather

**meteorologist**   a scientist who studies the weather and climates

**methane**   a gas formed from decaying plant matter

**millibars**   the unit of measurement for atmospheric (air) pressure

**molecule**   a tiny particle of something made up of a small number of atoms. A molecule of water, for instance, is made up of two atoms of hydrogen gas and one atom of oxygen gas

**monsoon winds**   winds that blow around the Indian Ocean, towards the south-west in the winter, and towards the north in the summer, when they bring rains and often hurricanes

**oceanographers**   scientists who study the sea and oceans

**oceanographic data**   facts and figures relating to the sea

**ozone**   a layer of protective gas 10–50 kilometres (about 6–30 miles) above the Earth's surface

**radar**   high-powered radio pulses reflected off objects to give an idea of their position and shape

**radiate**   to send out rays of light or other energy

**radiation**   energy given out by the Sun or the Earth

**Saffir-Simpson hurricane scale**   a scale for measuring different levels of hurricane damage and different levels of air pressure within the hurricane, usually, the lower the air pressure, the more severe the hurricane damage

**sandblasting**   when wind blasts rough sand against buildings or structures, scouring away the surface

**sanitation**   drainage systems for human and household waste and water

**spawn**   mate and lay eggs

**storm surge**   a huge wall of water created mostly by high winds cutting into the sea

**stratosphere**   the layer of atmosphere (band of gases) above the troposphere

**subcontinent**   a large land mass sticking out of a continent – subcontinents were often formed separately millions of years ago but were then fused with the nearby continent

**tornado**   a violent twisting, sucking wind that rotates around a funnel of very low air pressure

**Tornado Alley**   the vast stretch of land in the United States over which tornadoes commonly strike, running from the Gulf of Mexico in the south to the Great Lakes in the north

**tropical cyclone**   the technical name for a hurricane, used in Australia and on the Indian subcontinent

**tropopause**   the layer of atmosphere (layer of gases) between the troposphere and the stratosphere

**troposphere**   the layer of atmosphere (band of gases) closest to the Earth

**turbulence**   where air is forced to rise or descend rapidly it forms eddies and choppy waves, just like a stream when water is forced around a rock

**typhoon**   the technical name given to hurricanes around the western Pacific, China and the islands of Japan

**ultra-violet rays**   light outside the range of visible wavelengths, that comes from the Sun

**Venturi effect**   how the wind is channelled through, and made stronger by, narrow city streets lined with high-rise buildings

**vortex**   a fast twisting funnel

**water cycle**   the Earth's supply of water recycled in different forms as water vapour, rain, sleet, snow, hail and ice

**water vapour**   water in its gaseous state, heated enough so that it changes into a gas

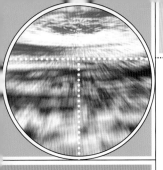

# Index